Winning Snooker

Winning Snooker

by W. G. Clifford
Edited by Geoff Martin

W. Foulsham & Co. Ltd.
London · New York · Toronto · Cape Town · Sydney

W. Foulsham & Company Limited,
Yeovil Road,
Slough,
Berkshire SL1 4JH

ISBN 0-572-01148-2

Photoset by Rowland Phototypesetting Ltd,
Bury St Edmunds, Suffolk.
Printed in Great Britain by
St Edmundsbury Press, Bury St Edmunds, Suffolk.

Contents

Chapter 1

Opening-up

There is an art to everything in snooker, and that includes the very first task that any player will be called upon to perform – spotting the balls. Spotting the balls is the term given to placing each of the balls on their designated spots prior to starting play, and nothing creates a worse first impression than to see the colours placed on the table slightly out of position. Be neat and precise in everything associated with the game, and it will pay dividends.

Spot the balls as follows – black on the top spot farthest from the baulk line, pink on the pyramid spot, blue on the centre spot, brown on the centre spot *of the baulk line*, yellow on the right-hand spot and green on the left. The fifteen reds are arranged in a pyramid with the help of a triangle as in Diagram 1. The ball at the apex of the pyramid should be as near to the pink as possible without them actually touching – take care on this point.

The scoring system is as follows: one point for each red, two for yellow, three for green, four for brown, five for blue, six for pink and seven for black. After pocketing a red, any colour can be taken. The game continues with alternating reds and colours until all the reds have been pocketed, a player pocketing a red continuing to take reds followed by colours until he fails to score. The colours, unlike the reds, are returned to their spots after pocketing until all the reds have been cleared.* The colours are then taken in order, starting with the lowest-scoring colour (yellow) and finishing with the highest-scoring colour (black).

If you are a budding world champion you may well have 'cleared the table' with a possible total score (or 'break') of 147, consisting of 15 reds, 15 alternating blacks, then yellow, green, brown, blue, pink and black in the required order.

This, understandably, does not happen often, even among the game's highest-paid professionals, and even when it does, it is not the highest possible break, for if your opponent misses all the balls with his first shot but leaves the cue ball behind a colour – a foul snooker – you are left a 'free' ball as penalty against him. You could then begin your break by potting any colour counting it

*The exception to this rule is the final red; if it is potted by a foul shot, it is returned to the table and occupies the black, or the next highest available position.

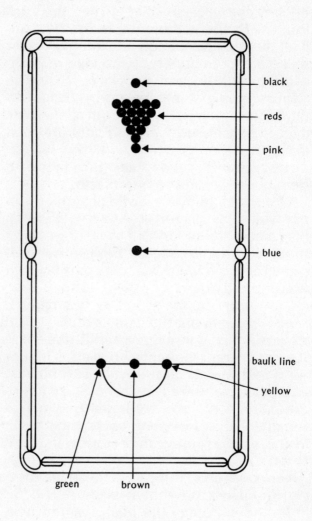

Diagram 1

as a red, followed by the black, and then go on to make a 147 break to give a total of 155. As this cannot be achieved without the generous co-operation of your opponent, and as I doubt whether even the likes of Hurricane Higgins, Terry Griffiths and Ray Reardon have ever achieved it in their star-studded careers, I think we need bother no more about that particular circumstance.

However, do remember the 'free ball'; it is an important and often misunderstood part of the snooker rules. Other less well-known rules will be dealt with as you would encounter them during the course of a game.

If you look at Diagram 1, showing the balls positioned at the start of a game, and suppose that your opponent takes the opening shot, miscues and contrives to miss every ball, what is the next stage? Some may argue that the game cannot begin until a ball is struck and that your opponent must therefore play again, but the official rule is that your opponent is penalised four points – the minimum penalty for a foul shot. You must take your shot from where the white ball, the cue ball as it is called, has come to rest. If you are snookered for the reds (in other words, cannot see a complete red) you may take a colour as a free ball, counting it as a red.

It is quite possible that with novices, games may well begin in this manner, but a steady improvement in the standard of the players will almost certainly rule such a beginning obsolete.

Let's take a more conventional start. Suppose you have the opening shot. You can place the white ball anywhere within the 'D', and a variety of shots can be played. Diagram 2 shows an opening shot that leaves little to chance. You play a shot parallel to the longest sides to clip the outside red, and strongly enough to bring the cue-ball round the back and a side cushion to snuggle against the baulk cushion. Cue freely and smoothly – don't 'jab' at the shot. An alternative is to spot the cue ball well over to the right and play at the outside ball on the second line of the pyramid, bringing the white round for safety as much as before. This breaks one or two balls away from the pyramid and should leave something worthwhile to aim at if you are first to start a break after the usual exchange of opening safety shots. That's all very well when you can count on making a useful break if the opening arises, but for openers the Diagram 1 shot is better.

Another quite feasible opening shot is to play to leave a snooker behind the brown instead of running along to the cushion but it is a difficult shot and if it fails, your opponent might be better placed than if left with the cue ball against the cushion.

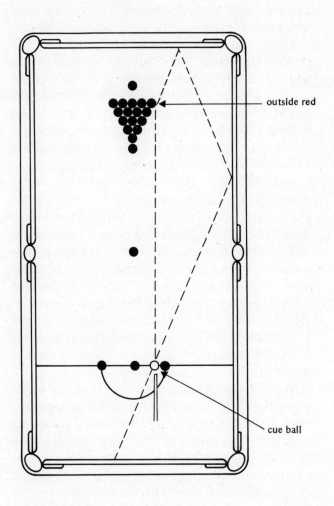

outside red

cue ball

Diagram 2

To make the point – never think about scoring with your opening shot. The only possible chance is a crashing shot off the top cushion, smacking hard and full on the second ball from the end of the row at the base of the pyramid. In theory, if the reds all touch each other and the pyramid is set correctly to a fraction of an inch, this shot should plant a red in a middle pocket. In fact the only certain thing is that the reds will be scattered to every corner of the table.

You may see this shot played in clubs when an experienced player is up against a relative novice who may be unable to cash in on the loose reds, but that doesn't mean it is a good shot. It simply pays him in such a case to have a bang and leave plenty of reds on, even if he doesn't pot one with the opening shot. The odds are that the more inexperienced player will soon make a mistake and the experienced player then has plenty of scope to make a big break, but against a better player this could be disastrous.

Points like this are, I think, important because they introduce the tactics of the game, and help players to consider every shot and its effects on the course of a match. This means a great deal in snooker. Obviously you must pot the balls to win, but it does not necessarily follow that the best 'potter' is the best player. Astute tactical play is more often than not the decisive factor, and this was indeed a feature of Canadian Cliff Thorburn's game when winning the 1980 World Professional Championship.

Speaking of professionals, you should be careful about relying on how much you may *think* you know after watching the great players. See them as often as you can. Happily, the media coverage of snooker makes this easy, and nothing can be more constructive or stimulating than watching the experts in action, but remember that they must make big breaks to win. Often they will pot a ball to keep a break going when, in the same position, a lesser player ought to treat the situation with more respect and play safety first. Trying to copy the professionals may prove expensive, and leave your opponent a good opening.

Remember this and you will be much more difficult to beat. It is usually as simple and easy to play for safety as to risk the shot which a player like Alex Higgins will pot with extreme aplomb.

Chapter 2

The tactics of snooker

Time and again shots will be played for safety, especially in the early stages. This 'sparring' for an opening is more important than it may appear, as the first mistake often allows the opposing player in for a decisive initial score.

Take care, and never be in two minds when you play your shot. In football a player taking a penalty kick is told to make his mind up before he strikes the ball, and the same rule most certainly applies in snooker. Settle down to play with deliberation for safety, or with equal deliberation to score. Seeing that first ball drop into a pocket may only be worth one point on the scoreboard, but it is worth much more in terms of confidence, assuring you that you are 'on form' and ready to score well. A bad first shot does exactly the opposite.

An exception is the 'ball to nothing' situation, when an attempt at a risky pot is justified because you know that the balls will run safe if you fail. Such a situation is illustrated in Diagram 3. Your ball is left as shown, and up the table there is a loose red which with

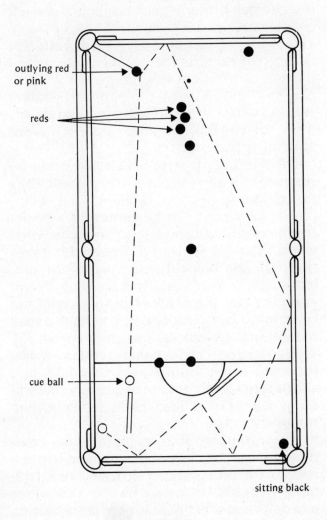

outlying red or pink

reds

cue ball

sitting black

Diagram 3

care can be cut into the top left pocket, with the cue ball brought back just below and left of its starting position, near the cushion. This is obviously not a shot you can attempt with great confidence, as even the best of players can miss at this range. But you can play thin and sharp on the right of the target red and with a shade of luck it may go down; if not the cue ball should be left in a reasonably safe position.

This kind of opportunity should never be ignored as it gives you a sporting chance of a score. Plenty of these openings will occur, particularly near the beginning of a game, but be ready to capitalise at any time, even when the table is cleared of everything save the pink and black. If you imagine the outlying red in Diagram 3 to be the pink, and suppose that the black is in the jaws of the right-hand bottom pocket, you have a 'ball to nothing' chance well worth considering. There is a good chance that if you fail to pot the pink it will bump away to safety, and should the shot come off, your cue ball will come round in an ideal position for potting the black.

It by no means follows that you are compelled to pot a colour if you happen to pot a red. Pause, and have a good look around the table. Should a colour be 'on' (in other words, seem a likely potting chance) with a chance for running up the table for another red, by all means take the opportunity. It is more likely, however, that you may pot green or brown in the middle pocket, although oblique shots into middle pockets are not to be undertaken lightly. The temptation to have a shot and perhaps get on to something up-table is strong, but before yielding to it, look around. You may see a colour, probably the yellow, resting near a side cushion, offering the chance of a good snooker which you could hardly miss – a much better alternative than those 'maybe' pots.

You can set up the snooker by rolling the cue ball directly and gently behind the colour, or instead you might play niftily off the cushion and directly behind a colour. 'There ought to be a law against it,' is what your opponent may well declare, but see how much better off you are by preferring the certain snooker to the problematical pot. Your opponent will do well even to hit a red, and at any rate he is likely to leave you an opening as safety will probably be the last thing on his mind. All he will want to do is get out of a nasty situation.

More often than not he will miss the reds and give four points away, very often presenting you with a clear opening into the bargain. He may even hit a big-scoring colour, boosting your score by seven if he cannons off the black, six for the pink or five for the blue, added to the possibility that either of these colours, having been moved, could be 'on' following the next red. Such things do happen, especially if your opponent is under pressure from a good snooker.

On balance there can be no question that the snooker will show a consistent profit if you make a habit of playing it instead of taking chances, but even though this is the name of the game, such tactics are not always the most popular. However, leaving snookers out of the game and replacing them with a 'try-a-pot-every-shot' attitude destroys a keen battle of wits which can make the game so absorbing. Players who throw away snookering opportunities for the sake of pocketing balls are at a distinct disadvantage, and will soon realise it.

On the other hand, there is little merit in 'cushion crawling'. By all means go for the pot – even a difficult chance – if there is really nothing else worth attempting, but never throw away an advantage by potting balls and shutting your eyes to the possibility of a snooker. This is perhaps even more vital in the late stages than at the start of a game.

Cool judgement is always necessary when the last red is left on the table, as many important matches have been thrown away through an error of judgement at this stage, leaving the last red and the colours on for an eager opponent.

In a recently televised tournament a player of some repute completed a useful break by taking the last but one red and leaving the cue ball between black and the top cushion, offering an awkward pot-black into the middle pocket. It was one of those times calling for a slowly played shot with allowance for the curl of the ball against the nap of the cloth near the pocket opening. The attempt to pot failed, leaving black exposed near the middle pocket and a relatively easy shot at the last red. This was put down by the opponent who took black, yellow, green and brown before playing a safety shot, so far in front by this stage that the game to all intents was beyond the first player's recall. That questionable attempt to take black in the middle pocket presented an opening which should never have occurred. The more obvious shot was to roll the cue ball behind black, which would have created a near-impossible snooker.

No apology is offered for dealing so closely with tactics at this early stage, for what is the use of telling you about scoring shots and sequences and dismissing safety in a few incidental remarks. This can only result in adding you to the host of badly balanced players who give away points galore because they have no idea of the occasions when safety pays best of all. Contempt for safety and snookers amounts to no more than lazy thinking and shabby tactics. It is in fact so simple to play only a potting game that it devalues what has rightly become a highly skilled sport. It simply isn't snooker, and any reader content to persevere with a 'pot-the-balls-and-leave-it-at-that' attitude is unlikely to benefit further from this publication.

Chapter 3

Doubles and pots

Before dealing in general with the shots known as 'doubles', I want to mention one which falls into the category of the 'ball to nothing' shot. It is that good old life pool shot affectionately known as the 'Cocked Hat' double, and is shown at the baulk end of Diagram 4. The shot may strike you as more lucky than reliable but this is a rash conclusion as some of the old 'pool hands', not without justification, will swear that it is pretty well an even-money chance.

The beauty of the 'Cocked Hat' is that it leaves the cue ball awkwardly near a cushion, and is extremely unlikely to leave the target ball dangerously near a pocket. Play it by hitting your cue ball low (so that it comes to rest after hitting the red) and hard and striking the target ball full on. It will flash away over the path shown by the dotted line to find the middle pocket as indicated – rather spectacular, isn't it? Inaccurate ball-to-ball contact may fluke the target ball into the top pocket instead and you may learn something about playing the all-round 'Cocked Hat' double into a top pocket. The general idea is similar to the shot in the diagram, but the lie of the balls is wider. It is less likely to be successful than the shot in the diagram, but it is nevertheless useful to know something about, as nine times out of ten it may leave the cue ball tight against the cushion at one end of the table and the target ball dead safe at the other. At best it will take a very good shot to pocket the target ball after this shot has been successfully played and, in the end-game, with the scores close and only pink and black remaining, a good 'Cocked Hat' shot can prove decisive.

Now let's try to score a few points, as the professionals might say when anticipating a break of 50 or more. Snooker is so full of variety, and there are so many individual shots, that your progress may depend on being able to approximate situations to those which will occur in the following chapters. The exact shot described in future diagrams will not usually turn up obligingly in actual play, but very often a closely related one will. Therefore if you have the diagram shots in mind to begin with, the problem can be solved with a little intelligent improvisation. When practising these shots it is useful to attempt variations, and quite possibly you may discover that the shot is not a variation at all, but belongs in a completely different category.

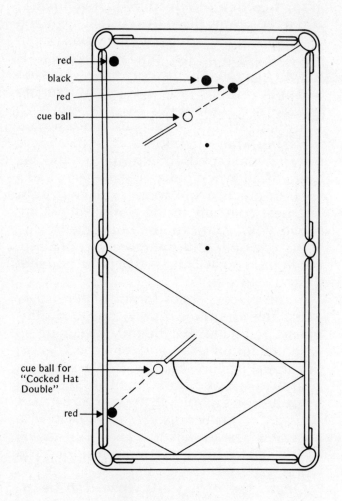

Diagram 4

23

Place the black ball on its spot as in Diagram 4, with a red dead in line with black, and a foot away. Place the cue ball eighteen inches from the red to offer a dead straight pot into the facing top pocket. The object is to stab that red into the pocket, leaving your ball exactly where red was, offering a certain pot-black to follow. Strike your ball now, sharp and straight. This is the one shot on the table where freedom of cue delivery is not recommended. It helps to hold the cue quite firmly when delivering the stab, and a spell of practice will soon produce results. The best coaching in the world will not improve your game unless you practise the shots yourself, and the more you practise, the better you will play – that is the one sure thing about snooker.

Some players seem to pot better if they grasp the cue quite firmly, but to do this means reducing that fluency of cueing so essential for billiards, and for a good deal of positional play in snooker. However, when all this is said and done, the balls must still be potted and if holding the cue hard makes you sure of many pots you might otherwise miss, it is best to stick to it and adapt as well as you can for more dexterous manipulation when required.

On to the next shot, which can be arranged by merely moving both the cue ball and target ball six inches closer to the top pocket, keeping them in exactly the same line as in Diagram 4. Now, instead of the stab shot, banging red into the facing top pocket, you require a six-inch straight screwback to pot red and leave yourself on for black. This is where the hard-handed cue grip can be a stumbling block, for while a certain degree of firmness in hold won't be a handicap, a really hard grip is fatal.

This is also the case with the next practice shot. Arrange this by simply moving the cue ball and the red six inches nearer to you than in the Diagram 4 stab shot. You now require an easy, straight follow-through to pot red and leave the straight pot-black. Strike your ball centrally and smoothly, no 'top' is needed to achieve the gentle follow-through, but good judgement of strength is essential and practice will make perfect.

Well-judged strength, allied to accuracy, is the making of a good snooker player, and for that reason you should practise these three simple shots over and over again. First the stab, then the screwback, then the gentle follow-through, all played to leave the cue ball dead in line with the black on its spot. When a top player is on for a good break you will see them play these shots, or their close relations, time and again, and you will certainly appreciate the ease with which all three can be rearranged when settling down to a spell of steady practice.

Satisfy yourself by potting the black every time your stab, screwback or follow-through leaves the cue ball in the exact position you want, but don't be content with anything other than perfect position. Promise yourself never to pot the black unless you have earned the satisfaction by leaving a dead straight pot, and consider an easy pot that is not quite straight as a complete failure. Positional precision is well worth striving for and this is as good a way to start as any. These shots accustom you to operate at the profitable end of the table, and give you a useful feel for the lucrative red-black, red-black scoring sequence.

That red ball at the nearside cushion, top left pocket, helps you through the 'alphabet' of that series. Play from the lie of the cue ball as it would be left after a success with one of the three shots mentioned. This presents a straight pot-black into the facing top pocket. Your new problem is to score this and get on the remaining red to the best advantage. The stab won't do because it will leave the cue ball on the black spot where you don't want it, and the follow-through may leave a very thin cut which is barely on. Obviously you need the screwback, played freely enough to pocket the black and return the cue ball in clear command of the desired red.

If played well, this pot red should leave you on for the black again. Therefore, by steady application of the simple shots indicated at the spot end of Diagram 4, you can score a useful two reds and two blacks. In addition you gain a working introduction to the stab, screwback and follow-through shots, and learn to adapt the required strength for positional precision. Don't, however, expect to learn this in ten minutes, or even as many hours. Be prepared to spend just as long as it takes to master these basic but highly important skills. Patience will pay!

Chapter 4

Improving your average

Potting of the highest standard is a gift. Some players do it with a natural flair, others are as likely to miss as score, but the ability of all can be improved. In America, where they are very keen on statistics, they often refer to 'potting averages', and even the best must practise regularly to keep that average up.

Diagram 5 shows some useful shots which should help boost your personal average and make you a more accomplished all-round player. Place a red on the centre spot and practise potting it in the facing top pocket. Strike your ball centrally and don't be afraid to hit this shot quite hard. It is pointless to attempt these long shots with a soft action, the likely outcome being a sitting shot for your opponent if you miss. Play a sharp, clean and confident stroke which will send the red smartly into the pocket without touching the sides, and when you manage to do this more times than you miss, you can consider yourself a pretty good shot at the long pots. Stick to this routine and your reward is certain, but practice is essential. It is no good to read about the shot and play it over and over in theory, and then only in a match.

By way of a variation, try cutting the red into the left middle pocket as indicated by the dotted line. Played from the same spot as in the longer shot; this will give you experience of those fine cuts which will often present themselves, and which are very satisfying when potted. Don't expect to get this one every time, or even most of the time as it is difficult, but the practice will be useful.

For this shot, you must play very accurately at top speed to have any chance of success and, as easier cuts are taken at the same speed, the effort on the more difficult shot is well worthwhile. Unless you have your own table and a good deal of spare time it is, of course, not easy to arrange this practice but a good idea is to find a friend as keen to improve as yourself, book the quietest table you can find and take, say, a dozen strokes in turn at each shot, with the free person setting up the balls. You can even make a game of it by counting up successful shots if you are the type who needs an infusion of the competitive spirit. Keeping a record of your scores will also keep you informed of the gradual but certain improvement you are sure to make. Potting a ball

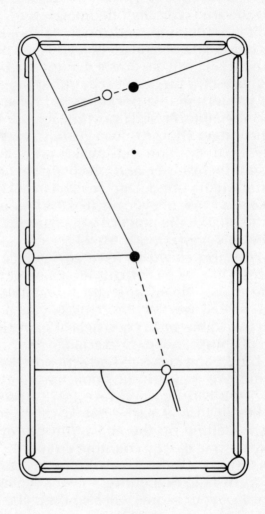

Diagram 5

without touching the sides of the pocket is a sure sign of an uncommonly good player, so cultivate the habit as much as you can. Often the lie of the ball offers an open pocket into which a ball will go even if directed decidedly clear of the pocket centre, but never be satisfied with this careless pot. Be adamant that nothing less than the centre of pocket is good enough for you and this will help your concentration on many difficult pots which must be dead accurate to succeed.

Pots to the oblique middle pocket will come off if a slowly moving ball takes the far jaw of the pocket before dropping in. If you play very steadily this enlarges the target, a point worth remembering when faced with a middle pocket teaser which is barely on. Don't forget that the merest graze on the near jaw of the pocket is fatal at any strength, so whatever you do, steer clear of that.

Continuing with the potting practice, it is time to introduce the spot-stroke, shown at the top end of Diagram 5. Play this shot however you like as far as practice is concerned. Slam it in, then trickle it so slowly that it barely goes down. Try variations of strength in extremes. The idea is to give you confidence when playing easy pots at any strength, a useful thing in the course of competitive play.

By varying the lie of the cue ball you can

set up an endless variety of pots off the spot. Such practice, while apparently straight-forward, is of immense value because you are working in that lucrative 'on the black' scoring zone. Never lapse into a casual at-titude here. Make a rule to mark spots for the cue ball for each shot, enabling you to play and replay your failures. When working at these variations from the straight pot it is a good idea to put a red where you ought to get on it after pocketing the black, helping to acquire the healthy habit of accumulating breaks. You pot black, get on red just right to take it easily and get back on the black. This is so important in the course of a game that a top player will be thinking as many as four shots ahead of the one he is actually playing.

Obviously, diagrams galore would be needed to show all possible variations from the straight pot, but it is best to work hard on your own weaknesses and use variations which might give you problems in the course of a game. Don't forget the change-over, practising from both sides of the table. Because the diagram shows the balls placed for set shots in one pocket, it does not mean that you should plug away accordingly. Simply reverse the lie of the cue ball and play into the opposite pocket, an indispensable aid. Neglecting it will make your potting ability one-sided and you will feel uncomfortable when potting on the side which is not your favourite.

In championships you will often see the experts study the line of the pocket, looking up and over to make sure of the line before settling down to the task of potting, particularly when the target is by no means tempting, even by their high standards.

Acting on the sound principle that what is good for the best must also be good enough for you, the advice here is to cast a careful eye over the line between the centre of the target ball and the centre of the pocket. Exactly how much value there may be in this ploy varies with the individual, but no doubt there are occasions when it is both useful and necessary. Use your own discretion. It is a waste of time to employ this tactic when you can see that the ball will go down nicely, but if unsure a steady glance over the line may make all the difference between pocketing a ball and bumping it against the cushion with a resulting miss.

Chapter 5

Sets and plants

Sometimes the shots in Diagram 6 are called 'sets'; other people call them 'plants'. It doesn't matter what you call them, but if you want to keep many a break going, you will have to be able to perform them. On the right of the spot end is the dead plant, a certain score whenever a line through the centre of both target balls ends in the pocket. The target balls must be touching as in the diagram. When the dead plant is clearly on it can hardly be missed, because it does not matter how you hit the nearest target ball, the other will be kissed into the pocket.

This makes the dead plant a shot well worth including in your growing repertoire. Take a careful look when you think a dead plant is worth playing and you will quickly see if it is on or not – the time is well spent. The shot is also on when you can force another ball against the target ball farthest from the pocket. Some special effects may result, and it is possible to play hard and shake up half a dozen or more bunched and touching balls to transmit enough power to plant one ball. All sorts of possibilities are likely to emerge if you disturb a bunch, either for yourself if you score, or for your opponent if you do not, but if you are well ahead it is worth taking an occasional chance with this spectacular shot.

The cannon plant shown top left of Diagram 6 is another with which to become familiar. You will see that an intervening colour bars a straight shot at the dead plant set for the top left pocket, but a simple cannon from red by-passes the problem ball as indicated by the dotted line. The cannon, of course, is essentially a billiard shot and a relatively easy one at that, but in snooker as a whole all sorts of billiard shots are in constant use. You need them positionally to build breaks, and defensively for 'snookering'.

Enjoyable snooker can be played by those who have never played billiards, but this type of player can usually be beaten by a potting equal who has the advantage of being also a useful performer on the billiards table. The link has been well established from the time Joe Davis was champion of both – around the same time that Kingsley Kennerley also won the amateur championships in the two games. Some may argue that snooker destroys your skill at billiards, but it seems a doubtful theory.

Snooker improves your potting at billiards. Your snooker improves from the knowlege of angles and cue ball movements which billiards alone can teach. A subtle blend of both games is therefore commendable, but it is a mistake to play one or the other game exclusively for weeks on end and then switch over, an action that would be sure to put you off your game for some time. By far the best plan is to mix billiards and snooker whenever you get the chance. Many players miss this point because with the recent upsurge of snooker as a professional, televised sport, their intention is to become proficient at this game only.

Back to the diagram, and a much more frequent use of the cannon in snooker is shown at baulk end (left-hand pocket). This offers a very simple pot-red into the bottom pocket, but it is by no means so easy to put that red down and at the same time execute the neat screw cannon on black which is necessary to position that ball over the other bottom pocket. Yet you must be able to play this kind of shot to keep a break alive, and there are many variations where a knowledge of billiards will help you to cope.

On the other side of the baulk is a plant which serves a double purpose. The actual plant, playing the near ball to kiss the far ball into the corner pocket, is simple enough, but the direct contrary is the case if we use the leave to settle an oft-disputed point in the free ball rule. Suppose that pink, the ball

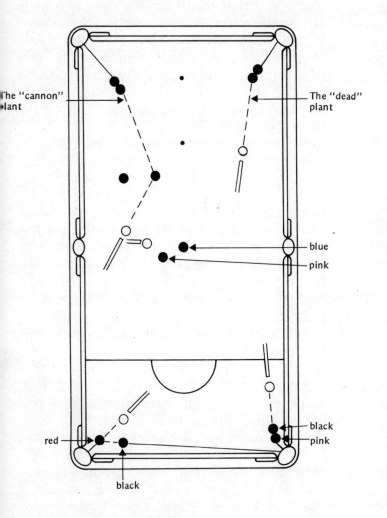

The "cannon" plant

The "dead" plant

blue

pink

red

black

black

pink

black

Diagram 6

37

which is on, is snookered by the intervening black and that these are the only two balls left on the table. The position has come after a foul shot, which means that the player at-table has a free ball. Obviously he can only hit black, but what is he permitted to do with it? The answer is that he can play black to plant pink in the pocket, scoring six for the pink and the black left on.

Suppose, however, that he contrives to pot both pink and black in the same pocket, with that one shot? He scores six for pink, which remains in pocket, but black is returned to its spot for his next shot. The point to remember is that the free ball offers the equal of two pinks on the table with black, the free ball, counting as pink without affecting the status of the true pink. If black had somehow been pocketed instead of pink it would still have counted as pink, the point being that both were on, as pinks, for the free ball shot.

At the centre of Diagram 6 is an arrangement of balls that should settle thousands of disputes as to what constitutes a 'free ball leave'. Blue, the on ball, is on its spot. Pink, the intervening ball after a foul stroke, barely covers the extreme right of blue. It is almost a clear ball, but careful sighting proves that it is not possible to hit any part of the blue directly. Consequently the player at-table has a free ball leave just as if he was snookered by pink. It makes no difference if, as often happens, an intervening ball does not prevent the ball which is on from being pocketed. After a foul, this is a free ball situation, and the player can please himself whether he pots the ball which is on, or takes another ball after nominating it.

But you are not allowed to snooker behind the nominated ball from a free ball leave. You may, however, play a cannon from the nominated ball to leave a snooker behind any other, which is often the best thing to do. You must always nominate whatever ball you may select as the free ball, but in the ordinary run of play you are not compelled to nominate your ball unless requested to by referee or opponent. The old rule that every colour had to be nominated no longer applies, but never allow this to make any difference to you when it is not obvious as to what ball you may be on when several colours are close together. Without waiting for a word from referee or opponent, say clearly which ball you are on. It's the sporting thing to do and there is still very much a place for that kind of attitude in snooker.

Chapter 6

Playing the double

Having been introduced to the 'Cocked Hat' double earlier, the way is clear for you to investigate the more usual double, no longer regarded as a fluke shot. A reasonable player can learn to pot them more often than not, and Alex Higgins in particular is a player who carries them off with spectacular verve.

The beginner must first avoid the common fault of playing his shot at the double with the intention of hitting hard enough to give the shot a chance off one or two extra cushions. With such a shot a score is most certainly a fluke, and no-one can guarantee exactly what will happen when you smash a ball hard against a cushion. This is because the force of the hit for a fraction of a second 'embeds' the ball in the rubber of the cushion, breaking the normal angle of return and making reasonable calculation impossible. This is self-defeating, as the precise calculation of angles is the secret of success at doubling.

Forgive me for introducing mathematics, but it works as follows: at normal strength

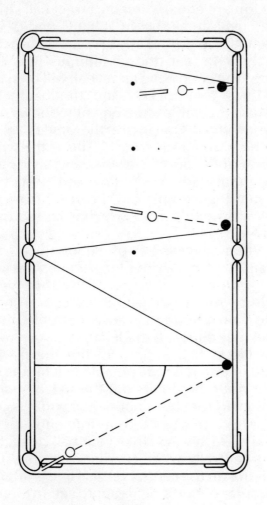

Diagram 7

the angle of incidence and the angle of re-flexion are equal when the target ball strikes the cushion, as shown at baulk end of Diagram 7. The dotted line shows the direction of the cue ball, the continuous line illustrates the course the target ball will then take towards the pocket, and the baulk line across the table conveniently shows at a glance how similar are the angles to the cushion and away from it. This is the whole secret of the double, a very exact shot needing great care in sighting and execution, something completely divorced from the 'hit and hope' stroke which is all too often played.

When the angle of rebound is very straight, as in the double further up the table in Diagram 7, the force of the shot makes little or no difference, an exception to the rule worth noting because a double of this type may appear a shade more certain when the target ball is flashed into the pocket. True or not, it is indisputable that hitting this shot quite hard cuts out the risk of a sitter being left for your opponent if you miss.

Unless positional requirements dictate otherwise, always strike your ball clean, true and centrally when playing a double. Low striking on the central vertical line is often an advantage, but 'side' is apt to set up all sorts of complications in ball-to-ball contact. The extent may not be noticeable but the deflec-

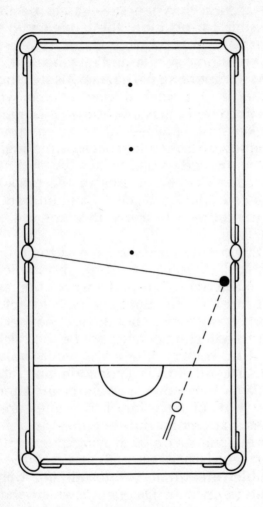

Diagram 8

tion may be just enough to spoil that essential accuracy. When side has to be used, possibly for position, the tendency to 'top your ball' must be avoided, for it will create unintentional swerve and ruin the shot.

At the spot end of Diagram 7 is – in theory at least – a corner pocket double which ought to be as playable as the usual middle pocket shot. However, these corner pocket doubles are less certain because the angle of entry into the pocket makes the shot more difficult. The target area of the pocket is reduced and it will take one-hundred per cent accuracy to carry this one off successfully.

Diagram 8 introduces one of the numerous 'cut doubles', a useful shot which is often the only chance of a score. The target ball must be cut thinly enough to get the correct angle of rebound for the pocket. Ball-to-ball contact must not be too thick as apart from the risk of a kiss, your shot will not succeed. This is a common fault, and it explains why some players never attempt this shot, or have forsaken it after unsuccessful attempts, but they may be able to correct the error by playing thinner than they feel is necessary. Sometimes the cut double offers that 'ball to nothing' opportunity shown in Diagram 9 which should never be ignored. Play as shown by the dotted line and the chances of doubling are good, by taking the target ball over the continuous line into the corner pocket. If your strength is right, no harm will be done if you miss. The strength of the shot should be sufficient to bring the cue ball back to the baulk, and at the same time bump the target ball well clear of the top pocket if it fails to drop in the pocket.

Many extremely useful safety shots depend on the principle of the cut double, combining safety with a chance of scoring. For a typical example, imagine the shot as similar to that in the diagram, with the addition of plenty of balls on the table, one or more of which blocks the pocket for the double. If you play as shown for the cut double you play the best shot, which is to leave the balls safe.

Obviously the assumption must be that the target ball is the only one open to attack – as will often be the case when many reds are bunched to the left. In these circumstances never try the direct pot into the top left-hand pocket. You may be tempted, especially if black is on its spot and able to be potted if you can sink that red, but you will do well to carry it off once in the proverbial hundred attempts. The odds most certainly are that you will miss the pot and leave something easy for your opponents.

A far better play, as indicated, is to try and leave the cue ball as near the baulk cushion

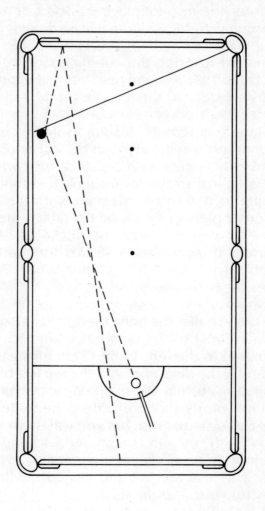

Diagram 9

as possible, keeping a wary eye on a red in the baulk if one happens to be there. Should that be on but snookered for you, your cut double for safety may be doomed to disaster. Consider instead a roll-up at dead (ie soft) strength on the bunch. It's not the cleverest of shots, but even the professionals will play it when nothing else is left. This may leave your opponent an easy safety shot which places you at a disadvantage. Left close to so many reds he will surely graze one and leave you with plenty of space to cover for your next shot, although occasionally he may contrive a clever snooker. There is also the possibility that the roll-up may leave a red exposed which, while not always apparent, is there every time for a keen-eyed cueman who knows what can be achieved when cue ball and target ball are close together.

These drawbacks are highlighted because so many inexperienced players regard the roll-up as cast-iron safety on bunched reds, often making this the beginning and the end of their safety play but, while necessary at times, it is by no means a sound shot.

Chapter 7

Building a break

Basically there are two ways of putting a useful break together – the right way and the wrong way. By the latter I mean potting ball after ball without the slightest regard for position. This can be very spectacular, but even the fastest 'breaksman' of modern times, Alex 'Hurricane' Higgins, does not go about things in this dashing manner unless in the mood to display some of those marvellous individual shots. For every break even he makes like this, hundreds are made through good positional control.

This means adding control of the cue ball to the pocketing of the target ball, even if it means at least doubling the work. Remember those stab, screw and gentle-follow pots you practised, as you will need them constantly to build breaks in the right manner.

For instance, at top left of Diagram 10 is a simple pot-red into the facing top pocket. But you need to play it with enough screw and side to get on black, lying below the right-hand middle pocket. Even then, you must get on black in a precise way. You must make the cue ball cannon on those two reds

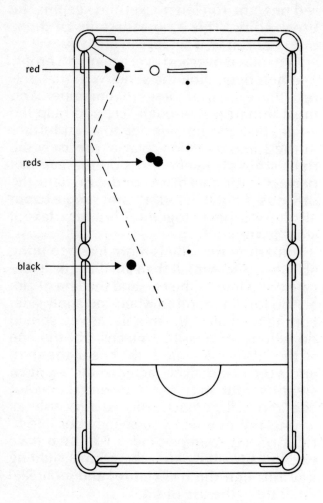

Diagram 10

near the pyramid spot, leaving the furthest red near the top left pocket and keeping the break going. This is no easy series of shots, but regard it as a set lesson and you will be able to play it over and over again with profit.

When beginning the series with that pot-red, there are four things to remember. You must impart just enough screw to help the angle, just enough left side to assist further in the same direction, play at precisely the right strength needed to stop the cue ball perfectly for the black, and – to state the obvious – pot that red! It's not simple to put all these aspects together, but let's take it step by step.

Imparting the side is more likely to bring about your downfall than anything else, because the line of the cue and the line of aim are no longer identical when you apply side. Hitting the ball in the middle, as you should do whenever possible, means that the line of the cue is the same as the line of the shot, and you instinctively acquire the habit of sighting your shot from the central point of cue-and-ball contact. This is obviously all wrong the moment you swing your cue to right or left to impart side. You then have two lines to allow for – the normal sighting line through the ball centre, and a parallel line due to the use of side.

This can be difficult, particularly when position demands as much side as you can obtain on the cue ball. The only solution, as always, is to practise the shot. Spot the ball on the top spot and pot it into the facing top pocket with an abundance of side on the cue ball, starting with the straight pot at a range of about eighteen inches and continuing until you have moved the cue ball its own width by degrees to the right and left of the straight pot. Then you will feel more confident about potting a ball no matter what side the cue ball may be carrying. At first, even if you pot well, you may be astounded to see how often you can miss even the dead straight pot when maximum side is applied.

To continue the set lesson, note carefully that the exact leave in the diagram demands the cue ball placed beyond the black, just where you can pocket it and cannon the two reds. It is not enough to leave a simple pot-black. In fact, to your probable horror, you must regard this as a bad shot! Screw and side give you direction, but correct strength needs to be applied to stop the cue ball in exactly the right position.

To be candid, perfect control of strength is more of a gift than anything else, but don't despair! We can train and improve, and it will do nothing but good to plug away at leaving the cue ball in a commanding position for the black.

The importance of this play is shown by the common end-of-game power in Diagram

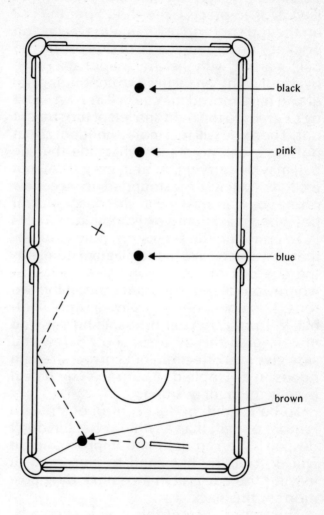

Diagram 11

11. Here you have brown offering a fairly easy pot in the bottom left pocket. All too easily brown can be sunk and the cue ball left anywhere up the table, but the one shot you are after must leave the cue ball above, and commanding, the blue as indicated by the dotted line. The ideal leave presents blue offering a steady run-through into the middle pocket, leaving pink in line for the top pocket and eventually a sitting black.

Make a bad shot on brown by going beyond blue to the cross on the diagram and, while you may still be able to take blue without too much trouble, there is no chance of getting on the pink. As you play over this lucrative end-game break you will be struck by its family resemblance to the problem of getting on black (Diagram 10). By varying the line of brown, you can present any sort of positional shot, from a plain-ball pot demanding nothing more than accuracy and strength to achieve the desired leave, to the most difficult of shots demanding screw, side, run-through and side, or screw without side.

Again the importance of solo practice cannot be overstressed and such practice must always keep the break in mind. If you pot a ball but find yourself out of position, start again. Adhere to this plan of practice until you can clear the table time and again.

A point often overlooked when playing a

colour during the course of a break is that it is some consolation that if nothing is left for you, the same applies to your opponent. You will often see hopeless attempts to pot a colour, notably black, without the slightest regard for the remaining reds. Worse still, this is often done when the simplest of shots on a colour would leave the reds safe. It may be that a snooker could be left if only that must-pot-colour craze could be forgotten. Nothing is more foolish than this sort of play at any time, but it is particularly ludicrous when a player has made a few points and takes a silly shot at a colour instead of playing a safety shot.

This is merely presenting the opposition with a present which may turn the whole course of the game, and is certainly not snooker as it should be played.

Chapter 8

The art of snookering

We don't call it 'snooker' for nothing. The art of the snooker is the distinguishing characteristic of a game which otherwise would only involve positional potting from beginning to end, varied only by safety play. Yet astonishingly there are still some players who feel reluctant to snooker their opponents. There is absolutely no need to feel in the least bit timid about trapping your adversary in the wiliest of manners, and it is a poor player who will not lay a snooker on for his opponent when he has the chance. One result of the increase in professional snooker is that it has helped players of all standards to become a little more ruthless as they inevitably seek to mimic the 'play to win' attitudes adopted by top players.

Diagram 12 shows an example taken from actual play. After taking the last red the player was left with all the colours on their spots, except green and yellow. Green was against the side cushion near the baulk line, and yellow was on the same side of the table, on the brink of the left middle pocket. The cue ball lay a few inches from the side cushion and a foot or so behind the cushioned green.

The player could have potted yellow easily and been left with tricky shots at some of the other colours. Instead, he wisely preferred to roll the cue ball gently behind the green to set the cast-iron snooker indicated in the diagram. A sound play, but rather distressingly there were murmurs among those spectators who have their own idea of what they call a 'sporting game'. In this position any player worth his salt should play the snooker, and so should you – without hesitation. Let's play sportingly by all means, but not to the exclusion of the use of cunning and subtle shots. The snooker should make you a better, and consequently more-respected, player.

Playing the snooker also shows that you respect your opponent, and are unwilling to yield anything to him whatsoever. It is as simple as this: in the example of play just described the correct shot, and the shot any serious player will employ, is the snooker behind green. From your point of view it could be the match-winner, as your opponent may well give four away in his attempts to overcome it, leave the sitting yellow where a cannon-pot on green is offered, and making the way clear for the potting of all the balls to the pink.

The snooker will at worst usually show a

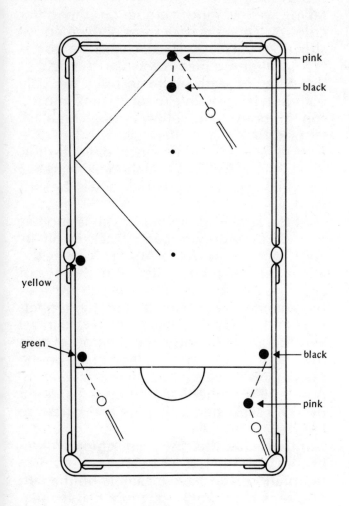

Diagram 12

57

profit compared with the risky exercise of taking yellow and getting on the other colours, and it is by careful judgement of situations such as this that games are won.

Another example is shown on the right of the diagram, with pink and black the only balls left. It is possible to smash pink into the top left pocket and follow through on black to position it over the right-hand middle pocket, but it is an extremely difficult shot. The simple follow-through pink leaves a convincing snooker on black, and is the shot to play.

At the spot end of the diagram is another not uncommon problem. Black is on its spot, pink is near the top cushion at the angle shown. If you fancy your chances of cutting a ball, the lie of the cue ball provides the chance to cut the pink into the top left pocket, but that pink has a long way to travel and the angle of entry into the pocket calls for a very exact shot. The least graze on the pocket jaw leaves a sitting pink for your opponent if no other ball interferes, as would be the case when only pink and black are left.

If this is not the case a similar leave often occurs with the last, or nearly last, red. The temptation is to have a gamble on the cut. The sensible thing is to ignore that temptation. Try instead for the one-cushion snooker behind black as indicated. It is quite a simple shot, needing nothing more than a steady follow-through on the cushion, designed to stop the cue ball behind black. This is not such an easy shot as the previous two snookers, but after a little practice it will be yours to call on whenever needed.

There are innumerable 'all-round' snookers, one of which is illustrated in Diagram 13. That's an unlucky number, and this will be an unlucky shot for you if you play it with the slightest hint of carelessness. The red near the top cushion is not on, and the cue ball is left in the baulk at the angle shown, so the shot is to play round as indicated to leave a snooker on one of the four colours clustered to the right. Don't hit that red too thickly. Clip it briskly about quarter-ball with plenty of left side on the cue ball. The shot is playable with surprisingly little effort but it does require a good deal of careful viewing beforehand. You may not always leave a snooker here but the odds are that you will, and the bonus is that whatever happens, you are sure to leave that red safe – provided you hit it with a shot of the correct strength. However, if your strength is inaccurate enough to spin the cue ball away towards the centre of the table, you will pay the penalty by possibly leaving it on.

In the left baulk corner is a snooker which should come into frequent use. The black here is what the great Joe Davis would have

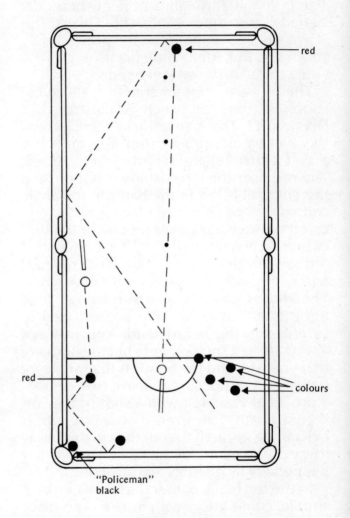

red

colours

red

"Policeman"
black

Diagram 13

called a 'policeman', barring entry to the pocket. Nor can you pocket that red just behind the baulk line. Instead, you are compelled to play the snooker off the red and neatly behind the colour.

You should bring the rest into use for this shot. In fact, never be too slack, lazy or shy to use the rest, 'spider', half-butt or long rest when the lie of the balls calls for these indispensable accessories. Countless games of snooker are lost by over-reaching instead of using the rest, so although it may be difficult to become acquainted with, it is well worth the effort.

Once you are accustomed to handling the rest you will find that the firm, unvarying bridge offered by the metal or plastic head is a help to potting, rather than the reverse, though this may not be your first impression. This applies particularly to plain-ball shots and little screw shots, both of which can be carried off with accuracy with the rest when they may provide problems without it. In fact, some find it physically difficult to provide high arches with the human hand, and in these cases the rest is just about invaluable. There is one more important point to remember when using any sort of rest: make sure that the hand, or the elbow of the arm holding the rest, is in contact with the table. This allows you much greater stability for the shot.

The stroke on the diagram is played fully on red, striking the cue ball with a sluggish delivery that gets weight into the stroke without the virile forward spin seen in ordinary play. Cue contact is central, or a little below. The sluggish cueing sends red off the bottom cushion as far up-table as you can manage, at the same time bringing the cue ball back off the bottom cushion to stop behind a colour.

Any number of variations are possible, sometimes at long range, but the principle is always the same. That slow run-through which gets the target ball well away every time, brings the cue ball back for the snooker you want. (The accomplished billiards player will see this as a cushion run-through played full at correct strength.)

One word of warning about snookers. Never snooker towards a pocket as, generally speaking, it is not wise to take the risk of playing a slowish shot at a ball which is on, with the object of sending it towards a pocket and setting up a snooker. An exception to the rule is the simple follow-through for an easy snooker. The trap to avoid is attempting to steer the target ball past another ball near the pocket to achieve the snooker. It will come off now and again but is too risky to be regarded as a utility shot. Better not to include this one in your rapidly increasing repertoire.

Chapter 9

Snooker and more snooker

One or two varieties of snooker are also popular, and all of them have a part to play in helping you master the endless variety of situations which will arise during the course of competitive play. Here is a description of three of the more popular variations.

SHORT SNOOKER

This can be played on the kind of undersize tables which are widely obtainable for a modest outlay. Tables of five or six feet in length usually have scaled-down balls, but it is difficult to get the feel of playing the real game because the 22 balls still crowd the available playing space. In short snooker only six red balls are arranged behind pink exactly as if the other nine were simply removed from the rear of the pyramid – that is, leaving only the first three rows. The game proceeds as normal and the shortage of reds makes no difference, except to the total possible score.

VOLUNTEER SNOOKER

This often appeals to those who relish a bit of a gamble on the table. The balls are arranged as usual. You pot a red to begin with then, as usual, you may play the colour of your choice. After taking this free colour, you may volunteer to pot any other colour instead of another red, as is usual. Should you succeed, you score the value of the potted ball, but if you miss, you forfeit its value. This is a highly entertaining game and it will help the inexperienced player get a feel for making big breaks.

REAL SNOOKER

Historians of the game reckon that this still-played variety of the 22-ball game is the original snooker from which the present-day sport evolved. It is played exactly as ordinary snooker in every respect until the point when all the reds have gone down.

Then comes the difference, and it's a big one. After potting yellow, the player may take any colour exactly as if he had just taken a red. After taking that free colour, he plays the green and, if successful, is again on any colour. The sequence continues: brown, any colour; blue, any colour; pink and black, taking the game to its conclusion. If a ball is taken as 'any colour' it returns to its spot; otherwise it stays down if potted.